OCT 2012

Stark County District Library
www.StarkLibrary.org
330.452.0665

DISCARDED
STARK COUNTY DISTRICT LIBRARY

D1472731

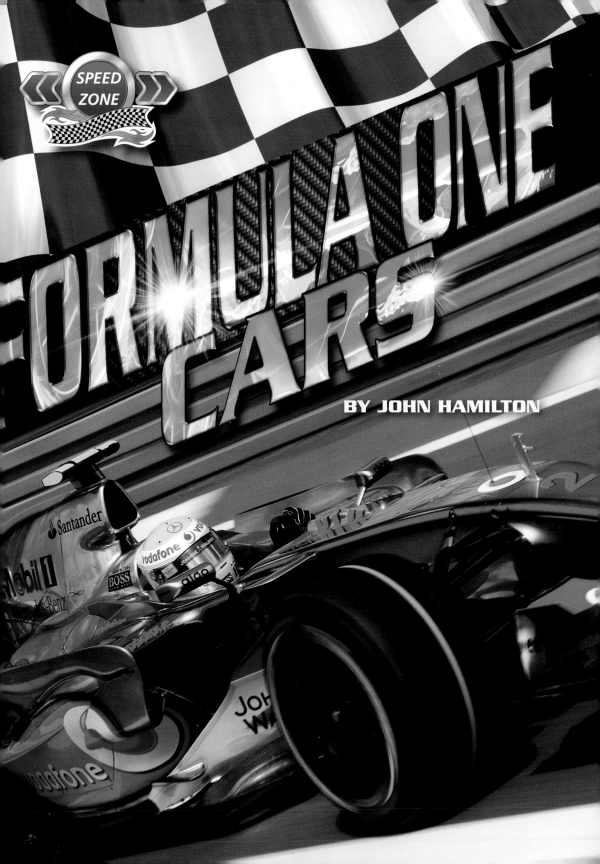

FORMULA ONE CARS

BY JOHN HAMILTON

VISIT US AT
WWW.ABDOPUBLISHING.COM

Published by ABDO Publishing Company, PO Box 398166, Minneapolis, MN 55439. Copyright ©2013 by Abdo Consulting Group, Inc. International copyrights reserved in all countries. No part of this book may be reproduced in any form without written permission from the publisher. A&D Xtreme™ is a trademark and logo of ABDO Publishing Company.

Printed in the United States of America, North Mankato, Minnesota.
032012
092012

 PRINTED ON RECYCLED PAPER

Editor: Sue Hamilton
Graphic Design: Sue Hamilton
Cover Design: John Hamilton
Cover Photo: Corbis
Interior Photos: Alamy-pg 29 (bottom left); AP-pgs 8-9, 10-11, 14-15, 18-19, 22-23, 26-27, 28, & 29 (top and bottom right); Corbis-pgs 1, 4-5 & 12-13 ; Getty Images-pgs 7, 16-17, 20-21 & 24-25; Renault-pg 6; Thinkstock-pgs 1 (Speed Zone graphic), 2-3, 30-31 & 32.

ABDO Booklinks
Web sites about racing vehicles are featured on our Book Links pages. These links are routinely monitored and updated to provide the most current information available. Web site: www.abdopublishing.com

Library of Congress Cataloging-in-Publication Data

Hamilton, John, 1959-
  Formula one cars / John Hamilton.
      p. cm. -- (Speed zone)
  Includes index.
  ISBN 978-1-61783-527-8
  1. Formula One automobiles--Juvenile literature. I. Title.
  TL236.H325 2012
  629.228--dc23
                                    2012008410

CONTENTS

FORMULA ONE

Formula One cars are single-seat racing vehicles. Formula One racing is also called Formula 1, or simply F1.

Formula One cars are the fastest circuit-racing cars in the world. They can race at speeds of more than 220 miles per hour (354 kph) on a straightaway.

XTREME FACT - An average season of Formula One racing is watched by more than 500 million television viewers worldwide.

HISTORY

The first Grand Prix race was held by the French *Automobile Club de France* in 1906. It was a 65-mile (105-km) course near Le Mans, France. The race lasted two days. Other races soon followed. They were held mainly in Europe.

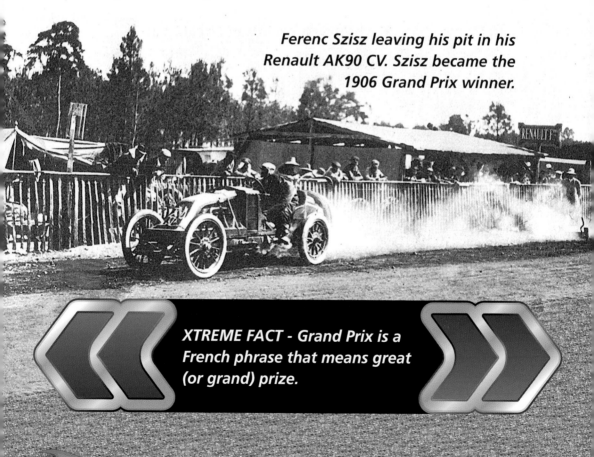

Ferenc Szisz leaving his pit in his Renault AK90 CV. Szisz became the 1906 Grand Prix winner.

XTREME FACT - Grand Prix is a French phrase that means great (or grand) prize.

Formula One racing grew from these early races. The first Formula One race was held in 1950 in England. Since then, Formula One races have been held annually in many countries worldwide. Even today, a Formula One race is referred to as a Grand Prix.

Giuseppe Farina taking a curve during the 1950 Grand Prix in England. Farina won the race in his Alfa-Romeo 158.

FORMULA ONE SEASON

Sebastian Vettel winning his second Formula One World Championship in 2011 in Suzuka, Japan.

Formula One teams compete in seasons. A season usually has between 15 to 17 races held all over the world. The races are called Grands Prix.

Sebastian Vettel's team also won the Constructor World Championship in 2010 and 2011.

Each team has two cars, plus drivers, mechanics, and other personnel. They come from many countries. Points are awarded for how each driver places in individual races. At the end of the season, the points are added up. Two World Championships are awarded, one for the best driver and one for the best team (called the "constructor").

XTREME FACT - An average Formula One team spends more than $120 million in a single racing season. Some teams spend much more.

9

CIRCUITS

Most Formula One racetracks, called circuits, are built just for the sport. Circuits are twisty, with chicanes and hairpin curves that challenge even the most skilled drivers. Large crowds of people line the raceway. An estimated 100,000 spectators attend each race.

XTREME FACT - Formula One races are usually named for the country in which they are held.

F1 racers taking a hairpin curve during the Monaco Grand Prix.

The race lasts about 190 miles (305 km), which takes less than two hours. A famous exception is the Monaco Grand Prix. It is 162 miles (261 km) long, and held in the streets of the city.

RULES

The "formula" in the name Formula One refers to a set of rules and regulations. These rules constantly change from season to season. The changes are sometimes made to help bring down costs. They also control the maximum speed allowed, which helps increase safety. Other rules affect a car's weight, engine, tires, fuel, and suspension.

XTREME FACT - *The organization that sets the rules in Formula One racing is the French FIA:* Federation Internationale de l'Automobile.

PARTS OF A FORMULA ONE CAR

Rear Wing

Engine Air Intake

Engine Air Intake

Bargeboard

Suspension

XTREME FACT - Famous
Formula One car constructors have
included Ferrari, Mercedes-Benz,
Renault, BMW, Lotus, and others.

Cockpit

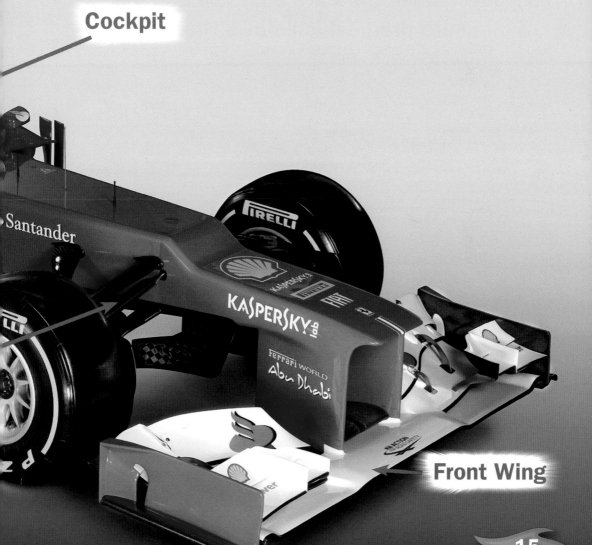

Front Wing

AERODYNAMICS

Aerodynamics is the way air streams around a vehicle. Teams spend millions of dollars designing cars with the best aerodynamics. Cars are built low and wide to minimize drag, which slows them down.

XTREME FACT - Formula One car chassis are made of lightweight composites and metal alloys.

Formula One cars have upside down wings in the front and back. They create downforce, which makes the cars "hug" the road. This helps drivers make sharp turns. At high speeds, a Formula One car has so much downforce that it could theoretically drive on an upside-down track!

A wind tunnel is used to test a Toyota F1 model's aerodynamic design.

OPEN WHEEL

Formula One cars are open-wheel vehicles. The wheels are outside the main body of the car. They are unlike street or sports cars, which have tires behind fenders.

Open-wheel cars are built just for racing. They use the most sophisticated technology available in motorsports. Open-wheel cars are lightweight for better handling, and the air rushing past helps cool the vehicles' brakes.

XTREME FACT - Open-wheel cars are also used in the Indianapolis 500. Indy 500 cars resemble Formula One cars. But Formula One cars are more powerful, with more advanced technology.

TIRES

Tires are an extremely important part of a Formula One car. Today's Formula One front tires are between 12 and 15 inches (30 and 38 cm) wide. The rear tires are between 14 and 15 inches (36 and 38 cm) wide. Different tread patterns are used depending on if the track is dry or wet.

XTREME FACT - Formula One tires wear out very quickly in a race, lasting only about 125 miles (201 km).

Formula One tires are made of soft rubber. When heated by racing around the track, the tires grip the road. This helps drivers make high-speed turns.

The front suspension of a Formula One car. This is adjusted before each race to make sure the vehicle responds to the driver's commands.

BRAKES AND SUSPENSION

Formula One cars use a double wishbone suspension. It connects the wheels to the chassis. The suspension includes springs and anti-sway bars that increase handling. Mechanics adjust the suspension before each race.

Formula One cars use disc brakes that are lightweight and resistant to wear and heat. They must help cars come to a stop from speeds over 200 miles per hour (322 kph). Air flowing over the open wheels helps cool the brakes. Brakes glow red-hot during a race.

ENGINES

F1 cars use 2.4-liter V-8 (eight cylinder) engines. They are lightweight yet incredibly strong and powerful. They produce about 750 horsepower. By comparison, a typical Toyota Scion produces about 160 horsepower!

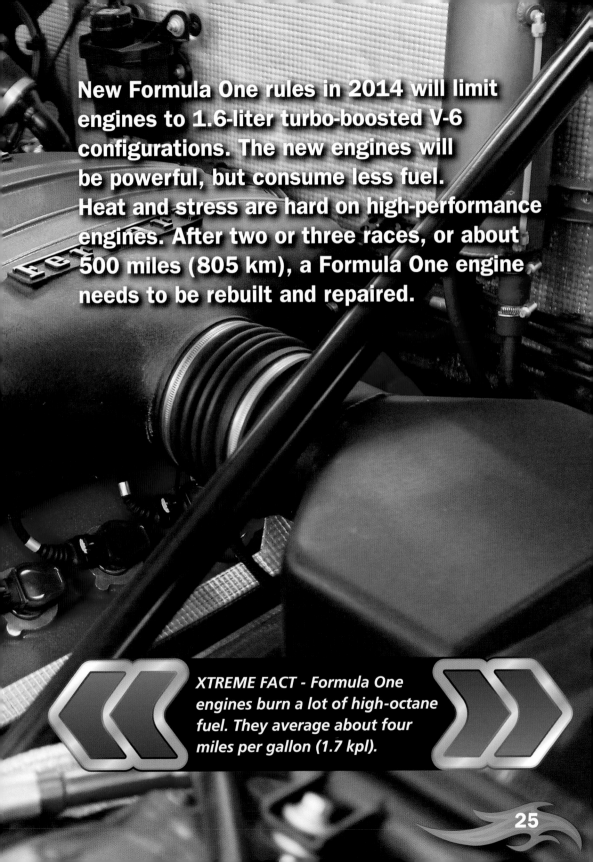

New Formula One rules in 2014 will limit engines to 1.6-liter turbo-boosted V-6 configurations. The new engines will be powerful, but consume less fuel. Heat and stress are hard on high-performance engines. After two or three races, or about 500 miles (805 km), a Formula One engine needs to be rebuilt and repaired.

XTREME FACT - Formula One engines burn a lot of high-octane fuel. They average about four miles per gallon (1.7 kpl).

COCKPIT

A Formula One car has a very small cockpit. It is just large enough to fit a single driver. No space is wasted. Seats are custom built for individual drivers.

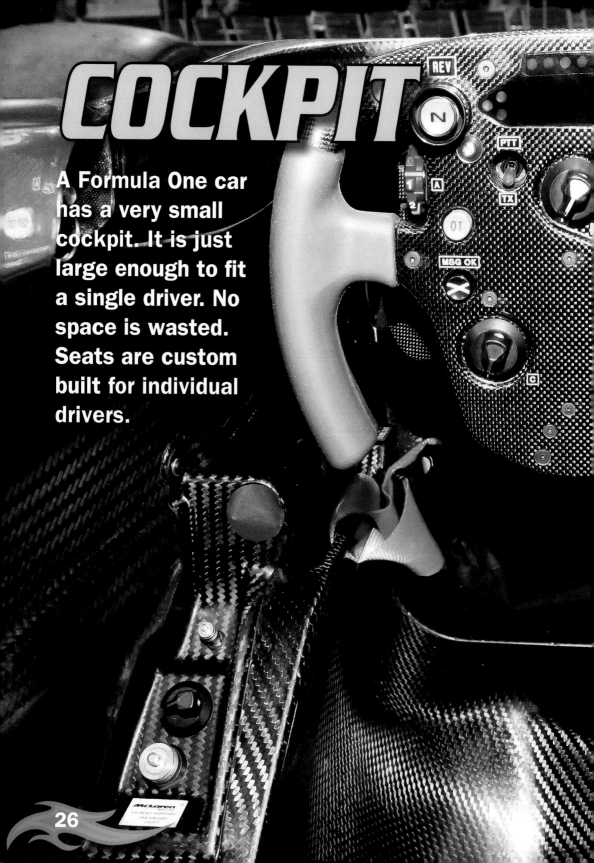

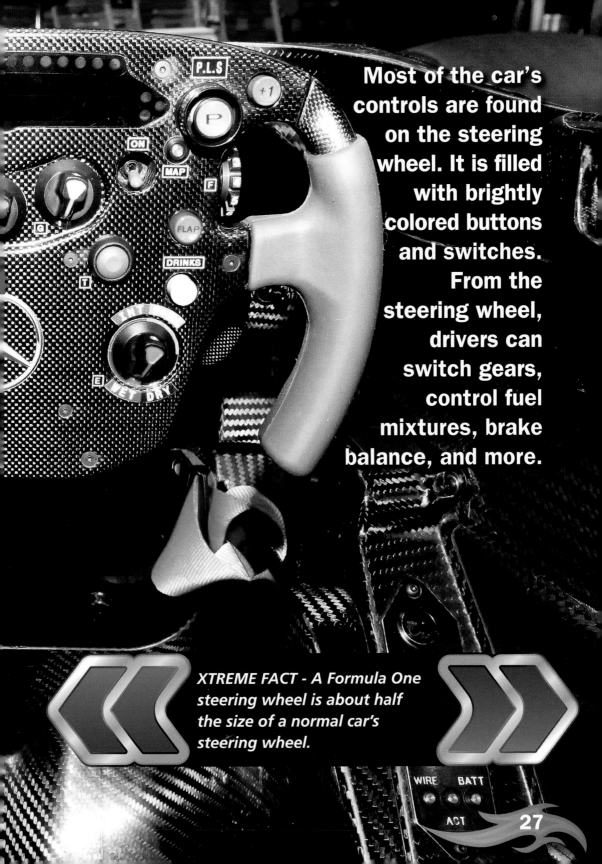

Most of the car's controls are found on the steering wheel. It is filled with brightly colored buttons and switches. From the steering wheel, drivers can switch gears, control fuel mixtures, brake balance, and more.

XTREME FACT - A Formula One steering wheel is about half the size of a normal car's steering wheel.

DRIVERS

Each Formula One team has two drivers. They are highly conditioned athletes. They have the reflexes and skills to control their vehicles. They also are very physically fit. Cardio conditioning gives them the stamina needed to complete long, high-speed races, often in very hot conditions.

Juan Manuel Fangio

XTREME FACT - Drivers must qualify for a special "super license," which allows them to race in Formula One Grands Prix.

Since 1950, Formula One has produced many champion drivers. Some of the most famous include Juan Manuel Fangio from Argentina, Michael Schumacher and Sebastian Vettel from Germany, Ayrton Senna from Brazil, and Scotland's Jackie Stewart, known as "The Flying Scot."

Sebastian Vettel

Michael Schumacher

"The Flying Scot"

Jackie Stewart

Ayrton Senna

GLOSSARY

Aerodynamic
Something that has a shape that reduces the drag, or resistance, of air moving across its surface. Racing cars that have aerodynamic shapes can go faster because they don't have to push as hard to get through the air.

Bargeboard
Pieces of bodywork attached to the sides of an F1 racing car to help with the aerodynamics of the vehicle.

Chassis
The body or frame of a vehicle.

Chicane
A sharp turn on an race course designed to slow down drivers.

Circuit Racing
A race on a closed track where racers all begin at once.

Composite
An artificially produced material that is made from two or more different substances. In auto racing,

many parts are made of composite materials that are strong and lightweight, such as fiberglass or carbon-fiber.

Hairpin Curve

A sharp curve in a road that resembles hairpins/bobby pins used to hold hair in place.

Horsepower

Horsepower is a unit of measure of power. The term was originally invented to compare the power output by a steam engine with that of an average draft horse.

Indianapolis 500

An extremely popular automobile race that takes place every May in Speedway, Indiana. As many as 400,000 people go to the Indianapolis Motor Speedway to watch the race, which lasts 200 laps. It is called the "500" because 200 times around the track equals 500 miles (805 km). The first Indy 500 was held in 1911.

Octane

A performance measurement of fuel used in internal combustion engines. A high octane number means the fuel will burn more efficiently. Racing gasoline with an octane rating of about 100 is often used in Formula One cars. In contrast, a street vehicle normally uses gasoline with an octane rating between 87 and 91.

INDEX